Copyright © 2011 XAMonline, Inc.
All rights reserved. No part of the material protected by this copyright notice may be reproduced or utilized in any form or by any means, electronic or mechanical, including photocopying, recording or by any information storage and retrievable system, without written permission from the copyright holder.

To obtain permission(s) to use the material from this work for any purpose including workshops or seminars, please submit a written request to:

XAMonline, Inc.
25 First Street, Suite 106
Cambridge, MA 02141
Toll Free: 1-800-509-4128
Email: info@xamonline.com
Web: www.xamonline.com
Fax: 1-617-583-5552

Library of Congress Cataloging-in-Publication Data

Wynne, Sharon A.
    PRAXIS Principles of Learning and Teaching (K-6) 0522 Practice Test 1:
    Teacher Certification / Sharon A. Wynne. -1st ed.
    ISBN: 978-1-60787-129-3
    1. PRAXIS Principles of Learning and Teaching (K-6) 0522 Practice Test 1
    2. Study Guides   3. PRAXIS   4. Teachers' Certification & Licensure
    5. Careers

Disclaimer:
The opinions expressed in this publication are the sole works of XAMonline and were created independently from the National Education Association, Educational Testing Service, or any State Department of Education, National Evaluation Systems or other testing affiliates.

Between the time of publication and printing, state specific standards as well as testing formats and website information may change that is not included in part or in whole within this product. Sample test questions are developed by XAMonline and reflect similar content as on real tests; however, they are not former tests. XAMonline assembles content that aligns with state standards but makes no claims nor guarantees teacher candidates a passing score. Numerical scores are determined by testing companies such as NES or ETS and then are compared with individual state standards. A passing score varies from state to state.

Printed in the United States of America   œ-1
PRAXIS Principles of Learning and Teaching (K-6) 0522 Practice Test 1
ISBN: 978-1-60787-129-3

Praxis Principles of Learning and Teaching (K-6) 0522
Pre-Test Sample Questions

STUDENTS AS LEARNERS

1. **Constructivist classrooms are considered to be?**
   (Easy) (Skill 1.1)

   A. Student-centered

   B. Teacher-centered

   C. Focused on standardized tests

   D. Requiring little creativity

2. **Mr. Rogers describes his educational philosophy as eclectic, meaning that he uses many educational theories to guide his classroom practice. Why is this the best approach for today's teachers?**
   (Rigorous) (Skill 2.1)

   A. Today's classrooms are often too diverse for one theory to meet the needs of all students

   B. Educators must be able to draw upon other strategies if one theory is not effective

   C. Both A and B

   D. None of the above

3. **Which of the following statements MOST explain how philosophy has impacted other subject areas such as reading, math, and science?**
   (Rigorous) (Skill 2.1)

   A. Most subject-areas emerged from Greek society and its great philosophers such as Plato and Aristotle

   B. Using philosophical arguments, experts have debated the best teaching strategies in various subject-areas

   C. Philosophy drives the motivation and dedication of most great teachers

   D. A majority of the 50 states require students to take several years of philosophical courses

4. You notice that one of your students is having a seizure, and her classmates inform you that this is because she was abusing drugs at her locker. What should you do immediately after contacting the main office about this emergency?
(Average) (Skill 2.1)

   A. Attempt to treat the student

   B. Find out the protocol for your school district

   C. Isolate the student until EMS or police arrive

   D. Interview classmates individually to gather the facts

5. This condition has skyrocketed among young children, usually presents itself within the first three years of a child's life, and hinders normal communication and social interactive behavior.
(Average) (Skill 2.2)

   A. ADHD

   B. Dyslexia

   C. Depression

   D. Autism

6. The difference between typical stress-response behavior and severe emotional distress can be identified by the:
(Average) (Skill 2.2)

   A. Situation, circumstances, and individuals around which the behavior occurs

   B. The family dynamics of the child

   C. Frequency, duration, and intensity of the stress-responsive behavior

   D. The child's age, maturity, and coping abilities

7. Which of the following does the least to address the needs of students with disabilities?
(Easy) (Skill 2.3)

   A. IDEA

   B. Title IX

   C. P.L. 94-142

   D. Least restrictive environment

8. **What is one of the most important things to know about the differences between first language (L1) and second language (L2) acquisition?** *(Easy) (Skill 2.5)*

    A. A second language is easier to acquire than a first language

    B. Most people master a second language (L2), but rarely do they master a first language (L1)

    C. Most people master a first language (L1), but rarely do they master a second language (L2)

    D. Acquiring a first language (L1) takes the same level of difficulty as acquiring a second language (L2)

9. **Which statement is an example of specific individual praise?** *(Average) (Skill 3.4)*

    A. "John, you are the only person in class not paying attention"

    B. "William, I thought we agreed that you would turn in all of your homework"

    C. "Robert, you did a good job staying in line. See how it helped us get to music class on time"

    D. "Class, you did a great job cleaning up the art room"

INSTRUCTION AND ASSESSMENT

10. **How can mnemonic devices be used to increase achievement?**
    (Average) (Skill 4.1)

    A. They help students learn to pronounce assigned terms

    B. They provide visual cues to help students recall information

    C. They give auditory hints to increase learner retention

    D. They are most effective with kinesthetic learners

11. **Learning centers are unique instructional tools because they allow students to do all of the following except?**
    (Average) (Skill 4.2)

    A. Learn through play

    B. Sit in their seats to complete assignments

    C. Select their own activities

    D. Set up the activity area under a teacher's guidance

12. **Discovery learning is to inquiry as direct instruction is to…**
    (Rigorous) (Skill 4.2)

    A. Loosely developed lessons

    B. Clear instructions

    C. Random lessons

    D. Class discussion

13. **A computer network includes physical infrastructure such as which of the following?**
    (Easy) (Skill 4.4)

    A. Software

    B. Web sites

    C. Operating systems

    D. Cables

14. **What would improve planning for instruction?**
    (Average) (Skill 5.1)

    A. Describing the role of the teacher and student

    B. Assessing the outcomes of prior instruction

    C. Rearranging the order of activities

    D. Giving outside assignments

15. Teachers must use lesson plans to do all of the following except:
    (Rigorous) (Skill 5.1)

    A. Meet specified goals and objectives

    B. Match the lesson to students' abilities and needs

    C. Test a strategy proposed by a research journal

    D. Meet state and local learning standards

16. Norm-referenced tests:
    (Rigorous) (Skill 6.1)

    A. Provide information about how local test takers performed compared to local test takers from the previous year

    B. Provide information about how the local test takers performed compared to a representative sampling of national test takers

    C. Make no comparisons to national test takers

    D. None of the above

17. _____ is a standardized test in which performance is directly related to the educational objective(s)
    (Rigorous) (Skill 6.1)

    A. Aptitude test

    B. Norm-referenced test

    C. Criterion-referenced test

    D. Summative evaluation

18. Which of the following is the least appropriate reason for teachers to be able to analyze data on their students?
    (Rigorous) (Skill 6.2)

    A. To provide appropriate instruction

    B. To make instructional decisions

    C. To separate students into weaker and stronger academic groups

    D. To communicate and determine instructional progress

19. **The seven purposes of assessment, they include all of the following except:**
    (Easy) (Skill 6.2)

    A. To identify students' strengths and weaknesses

    B. To assess the effectiveness of a particular instructional strategy

    C. To provide data that assists in decision making

    D. None of the above

COMMUNICATION TECHNIQUES

20. What has research shown to be the effect of using advance organizers in the lesson? *(Average) (Skill 7.1)*

    A. They facilitate learning and retention

    B. They allow teachers to use their planning time effectively

    C. They only serve to help the teacher organize the lesson

    D. They show definitive positive results on student achievement

21. To facilitate discussion-oriented, non-threatening communication among all students, teachers must do which of the following: *(Average) (Skill 8.1)*

    A. Model appropriate behavior

    B. Allow students to express themselves freely

    C. Show students that some views will not be tolerated

    D. Explain that students should not disagree

22. In diverse classrooms, teachers must ensure that they neither protect students from criticism nor praise them because of their ethnicity or gender. Doing either action may result in which of the following outcomes. *(Average) (Skill 8.1)*

    A. Classmates may become anxious or resentful when dealing with the diverse students

    B. Parents will appreciate their child being singled out

    C. The child will be pleased to receive this attention

    D. Other teachers will follow this example

PROFESSION AND COMMUNITY

23. **Teachers should network with one another for all of the following reasons except _____?**
    (Average) (Skill 10.1)

    A. To discuss challenges they face in their classrooms

    B. To develop a sense of community

    C. To earn their clock-hours for licensure renewal

    D. To find solutions to difficult problems

24. **According to research, one of the greatest obstacles facing new teachers is which of the following?**
    (Easy) (Skill 10.3)

    A. Behavioral issues

    B. Disagreements with the administration

    C. Excessive paperwork

    D. Fending off colleagues who give unwanted advice

Case History

Ms. Jones' Class

Ms. Jones is a new fourth grade teacher. She has 27 students in her class. Her school, Oak Street Elementary, draws from a wide variety of neighborhoods, and the students are very diverse. Some come from impoverished families and others from middle class families. There are almost an equal number of students who are African American, Latino, and White. A small remainder of students is from other racial groups.

The reading curriculum that Ms. Jones must teach is highly prescribed, meaning that over an hour and a half, she must follow the text, with all its activities, closely. Each week, the class typically reads a story together, and most of their activities are related to the story. On Mondays there is a heavy emphasis on vocabulary. Then students read the story for the first time on Tuesdays; they often re-read the story on Wednesday. Or, if it is a longer story, they will read the first half on Tuesday and the second half on Wednesday. Thursdays and Fridays are reserved for writing activities, vocabulary quizzes, graphic organizers, and other synthesizing assignments.

Getting to Know Ms. Jones' Students

Ms. Jones's class is intentionally heterogeneous, meaning that students in the class have varied achievement levels. Two students have been tested as gifted and are part of the school's Gifted and Talented Education program. Three of her students have Individual Educational Plans (IEPs), and one of these three has a behavioral disorder. He came from an abusive family and still suffers from the experience. The other two have Attention Deficit Hyperactivity Disorder.

Ms. Jones realized on the first day of school that some students were quiet and shy, while others were very social and talkative. She also noticed that some students were more motivated than others.

New Teacher Coach Observation Notes - Tuesday, October 14th

I like how Ms. Jones called the class' attention immediately after they returned from recess. She did a good job of getting everyone seated quickly. The students seemed to really know the procedures to get started with reading.

Ms. Jones quickly groups them into pairs. It appears that she has randomly assigned students together. I know two students who have IEPs, and they are together; yet another student with an IEP is matched with a gifted student. I'm not quite sure why she paired students this way.

First, the class reviewed yesterday's vocabulary words. It looks like some of the students do not remember the meanings of the words. I notice that two boys on the far left side of the room are play fighting with their pencils. I don't think Ms. Jones notices this. Ms. Jones says to the class, "Okay, let's start reading the story. Switch off when I flick the lights, okay." One person in each pair is reading aloud, while the other student is supposed to be following along. It looks like some are not. Furthermore, it is very noisy in the room now. I wonder how students are concentrating on the meaning of the story.

She flicks the lights, and students slowly switch to the other reader. It seems like a messy process. Some pairs switch immediately, right in the middle of the sentence; others wait for a more appropriate stopping point. They continue reading for a few minutes, and then Ms. Jones switches readers again.

At the end of the reading, Ms. Jones has a graphic organizer on the board. It is a flow-map. She asks each pair to join the pair next to them to make groups of four. These groups of four work on completing a graphic organizer until the end of reading time. Most groups are working productively, however, some barely finished in time; those who did not finish in time had flow-maps that were incomplete, messy, and occasionally incorrect.

Discussion between Ms. Jones (J) and New Teacher Coach (C) - Later in the Afternoon

C: What did you like about this lesson?

J: Well, I was glad that we got everything done today. I didn't think they'd be able to do both the entire story, as well as the graphic organizer. That's a lot of work for such a short period of time. I know everyone didn't do as well as I would have liked, but most of them did a great job.

C: Well, I'm glad you got everything done, but are you sure that all your students understood the story?

J: I'm pretty sure, as the graphic organizers look good.

C: But you had them in groups; how do you know all students understood?

J: I'm not sure.

C: I'm also wondering how well they knew the vocabulary words from yesterday. What did you do to connect the words to their background knowledge?

J: We did word webs. The students seemed to know the words quite well at the end of reading yesterday. I was surprised to see that some of them forgot the words today. I want to go over the words again tomorrow.

C: That's terrific! Now, did you notice that the boy in the third row, a little to the left, was a little confused? Is he learning English?

J: Oh, yes, that's Christian. He is a native Spanish-speaker. He's doing fine in English, though. I hear him talking in English proficiently with all his friends as if he were a native speaker.

C: Okay, but I'm concerned he did not know what he was reading today.

J: I better check into that.

C: I also noticed that a few groups were not working together well. It seemed that they were arguing over the paper being messy. Do they have strategies for dealing with disagreements in groups?

J: No, but usually, I try to monitor everything carefully. I must not have seen that. If I had, I would have dealt with it.

C: Well, we better end the meeting for the afternoon. Let's talk tomorrow about how we can fix some of these issues. You did great, despite the concerns I brought up. You're going to make a fine teacher!!

Ms. Jones' Teaching Journal - Tuesday, October 14th

There are a few things I'd do differently, but overall, I'm pleased with what happened today. I just don't know how to get through to Kelly. She seems very upset about something; obviously, her reaction to her group about the sloppiness on the paper was uncalled for. I suppose I may need to teach some better group behaviors. I hope to be able to work more closely with Danny. His IEP says he needs extra teacher-time, but I'm really struggling to get that time in there for him.

Question 1

Ms. Jones presented a well-planned lesson and used strong instructional strategies. However, she noticed that not all students responded to the lesson in the way she desired.

- Explain some of the elements of Ms. Jones' class that day that could have been modified to meet the needs of all students.
- Provide recommendations on how Ms. Jones can be guided by learning theories as she makes modifications to her lessons in the future.

Question 2

Ms. Jones' class is very diverse. She definitely wants to reach all students, but with 27 students in her class, she has to find ways to differentiate her instruction.

- Discuss aspects of Ms. Jones' lesson that could have been better differentiated.
- Provide recommendations using knowledge of classroom management, learning theory, learning English as a second or other language, and learning disabilities.

Question 3

Ms. Jones was concerned about the fact that some students had forgotten many of the words they studied yesterday.

- Discuss the importance of learning new concepts and vocabulary in context.
- Provide examples of how Ms. Jones might extend the students' learning of vocabulary throughout the week.

Case History

Scenario
Terrace Park Elementary has a tradition of assigning research reports in every class from grades two to six. In grades two and three, students explore topics and write paragraphs to demonstrate their new learning. In grades four and five, students learn conventions of research reports and practice using libraries and the Internet to do research. In fifth grade, students write a short report on a U.S. state. In grade six, students have to integrate all their knowledge of research reports and write a report on a U.S. president of their choice.

Mr. Michaels has taught sixth grade at Terrace Park for a few years. He has analyzed all aspects of his teaching each year and made changes to improve in subsequent years. His approach to this research report unit is no different; since this is the pinnacle of the sixth grade at Terrace Park, Mr. Michaels wants to make this project the finest instructional experience students have ever had at the school.

The Professional Learning Community of Terrace Park
All upper grade teachers at Terrace Park Elementary meet together every other week to plan lessons, discuss units, and design assessments. They often look at student learning data to guide their practices. Now that the teachers are getting ready to start the research report assignment in each of their classes, Mr. Michaels has compiled data from last year's assignment and developed tentative plans for this year's assignment. Other teachers have also brought in data and lesson plans.

During the planning meetings, teachers first examine the work of their current students when they were in the previous grade. So, Mr. Michaels spends this meeting looking at his students' fifth grade state reports. He also discusses his students' performance with their fifth grade teacher, Ms. Johnson.

Conversation between Ms. Johnson (J) and Mr. Michaels (M) - Prior to Starting the Research Assignment
J: I think you're going to find that your students really enjoy researching presidents. I'm not so sure that you'll be impressed with their skills in researching and writing reports. I know last year was the first time they had learned how to evaluate sources on the Internet, but I really don't think they got it at all.

M: That's okay. I plan on spending considerable time with that this year. What things did they master in terms of developing research skills?

J: Well, in the fourth grade, they had learned how to use the index of books. They really built on that skill last year. I doubt you'll have to spend much time on that. Last year, we spent a lot of time on learning how to summarize and paraphrase the research they find. However, I would argue that they have a lot of extra work to do with that, just because it is so hard. At this point, I really couldn't tell you how well they will do; all I know is that we spent a lot of time on it.

M: What about the writing of the reports? How well did they do with that?

J: Well, as you know, their skills in writing are all over the place. I think about half the class is at standard, one quarter below standard, and one quarter way above standard. It makes it very tough to teach to all students.

M: I hear you there! Thanks for all your advice!

From Mr. Michaels' Lesson Plan Journal - Prior to Starting the Research Assignment

I have yet to decide how I want to group students. I know that I am going to have to group them heterogeneously. I also know that I want to teach many concepts such as using graphic organizers to plan writing, assist in reading bibliographies, and revising writing. I don't know whether I should completely re-teach summarization, as Ms. Johnson did spend a lot of time on that. I'm a little concerned about some of the students who plagiarized on their science reports last fall. Maybe I should lay out the rules on plagiarism again. What I really want to focus on, though, is critical thinking. Unfortunately, the last time I did a critical thinking lesson, I don't think it went over very well. Finally, I hope I can find enough resources online and at the school library. I'll just jump into this and see where it takes me!!

A Day in the Life of Mr. Michaels' Writing Workshop - Half-way Into the Research Report Assignment

Students are in writing groups. Mr. Michaels just finished a mini-lesson on the differences between passive and active voice. In writing groups, Mr. Michaels has asked his students to read each others' papers and identify areas where passive voice could be changed to active voice. In one group, some students clearly did not understand the lesson and are now making other corrections to each others' papers, such as spelling. Mr. Michaels did not work with this group, as he assumed they were working on active and passive voice. One student in another group seemed to be struggling with coming up with an active version of a passive sentence. The rest of his group has left him behind as the rest of them seemed proficient with the concept. Since most of the class did understand the work for the day, Mr. Michaels' is concerned about whether or not he should return to this lesson the next day or move on.

Question 1

Clearly, Mr. Michaels wanted to understand where his students were prior to beginning this unit of instruction. He wanted to make sure he was starting at an appropriate instructional level.

- What additional areas could Mr. Michaels have investigated before planning this unit? What types of additional data could he have used to drive instruction?
- How could Mr. Michaels better monitor students' learning throughout the unit so that he is constantly aware of where they are? Base your answer on principles of instructional planning and assessment.

Question 2

Mr. Michaels was concerned about student plagiarism. He also expressed confusion over whether to re-teach skills such as summarization. Ms. Johnson suggested that the students did not have enough time to learn the skills of evaluating research sources, particularly from the Internet.

- Provide recommendations for Mr. Michaels as he decides instructional areas to focus on for this unit. Base your answers on knowledge of curriculum, instructional planning, and student learning.

Question 3

Mr. Michaels has some concept of what he wants students to do with this report, but he did say, "I'll just jump into this and see where it takes me."

- What problems might arise with this approach?
- How can Mr. Michaels retain the ability to utilize "teachable moments" while still holding students accountable to a clearly defined standard? Base your answer on theories of learning and assessment.

Praxis Principles of Learning and Teaching (K-6) 0522
Pre-Test Sample Questions with Rationales

STUDENTS AS LEARNERS

1. **Constructivist classrooms are considered to be?**
   (Easy) (Skill 1.1)

    A. Student-centered

    B. Teacher-centered

    C. Focused on standardized tests

    D. Requiring little creativity

Answer: A. Student-centered
Student-centered classrooms are considered to be "constructivist," in that students are given opportunities to construct their own meanings onto new pieces of knowledge.

2. **Mr. Rogers describes his educational philosophy as eclectic, meaning that he uses many educational theories to guide his classroom practice. Why is this the best approach for today's teachers?**
   (Rigorous) (Skill 2.1)

    A. Today's classrooms are often too diverse for one theory to meet the needs of all students

    B. Educators must be able to draw upon other strategies if one theory is not effective

    C. Both A and B

    D. None of the Above

Answer: C. Both A and B
No one theory will work for every classroom; a good approach is for an educator to incorporate a range of learning theories in his/her practice. Still, under the guidance of any theory, good educators will differentiate their instructional practices to meet the needs of individual students' abilities and interests using various instructional practices.

3. **Which of the following statements MOST explain how philosophy has impacted other subject areas such as reading, math, and science?**
   (Rigorous) (Skill 2.1)

   A. Most subject-areas emerged from Greek society and its great philosophers such as Plato and Aristotle

   B. Using philosophical arguments, experts have debated the best teaching strategies in various subject-areas

   C. Philosophy drives the motivation and dedication of most great teachers

   D. A majority of the 50 states require students to take several years of philosophical courses

Answer: B. Using philosophical arguments, experts have debated the best teaching strategies in various subject-areas
Academic subject-areas have also added to the philosophical debate on teaching. For example, reading teachers have long debated whether phonics or whole language was more appropriate as an instructional method. Language Arts teachers have debated the importance of a prescribed canon (famous works of literature) versus teaching literature simply to teach thinking skills and an appreciation of good literature. Math teachers have debated the extent to which application is necessary in math instruction; while some feel that it is more important to teach structure and process, others suggest that it is only relevant if math skills are taught in context.

4. **You notice that one of your students is having a seizure, and her classmates inform you that this is because she was abusing drugs at her locker. What should you do immediately after contacting the main office about this emergency?**
   (Average) (Skill 2.1)

   A. Attempt to treat the student

   B. Find out the protocol for your school district

   C. Isolate the student until EMS or police arrive

   D. Interview classmates individually to gather the facts

Answer: C. Isolate the student until EMS or police arrive
Never, under any circumstances, attempt to treat, protect, tolerate, or negotiate with a student who is showing signs of a physical crisis. It is advisable to find out the protocol for a particular school or district; however, most schools require the student to be isolated until they are removed from the school center by EMS or police.

5. This condition has skyrocketed among young children, usually presents itself within the first three years of a child's life, and hinders normal communication and social interactive behavior.
(Average) (Skill 2.2)

   A. ADHD

   B. Dyslexia

   C. Depression

   D. Autism

Answer: D. Autism
Educators and researchers are sensitive to all disabilities; however, the field has seen autism skyrocket among young children. This condition usually presents itself within the first three years of a child's life and hinders normal communication and social interactive behavior.

6. The difference between typical stress-response behavior and severe emotional distress can be identified by the:
(Average) (Skill 2.2)

   A. Situation, circumstances, and individuals around which the behavior occurs

   B. The family dynamics of the child

   C. Frequency, duration, and intensity of the stress-responsive behavior

   D. The child's age, maturity, and coping abilities

Answer: A. Situation, circumstances, and individuals around which the behavior occurs
Since all children experience stressful periods within their lives, from time to time, all students may demonstrate some behaviors that indicate emotional distress. Emotionally healthy students can maintain control of their own behavior even during stressful times. The difference between typical stress-response behavior and severe emotional distress is determined by the frequency, duration, and intensity of stress-responsive behavior.

7. Which of the following does the least to address the needs of students with disabilities?
(Easy) (Skill 2.3)

    A.   IDEA

    B.   Title IX

    C.   P.L. 94-142

    D.   Least restrictive environment

Answer: B. Title IX
The U.S. Constitution does not specify protection for education. However, all states provide education, and thus individuals are guaranteed protection and due process under the 14th Amendment. The basic source of law for special education is the Individuals with Disabilities Education Act (IDEA) and its accompanying regulations. After segregation was outlawed by the decision from Brown v. Board of Education, parents and other advocates filed similar lawsuits on behalf of children with special needs. The culmination of their efforts resulted in P.L. 94-142. The definition of a Least Restrictive Environment (LRE) differs with each child's needs. LRE means that the student is placed in an environment, which is not dangerous or overly controlling or intrusive.

8. What is one of the most important things to know about the differences between first language (L1) and second language (L2) acquisition?
(Easy) (Skill 2.5)

    A.   A second language is easier to acquire than a first language

    B.   Most people master a second language (L2) , but rarely do they master a first language (L1)

    C.   Most people master a first language (L1), but rarely do they master a second language (L2)

    D.   Acquiring a first language (L1) takes the same level of difficulty as acquiring a second language (L2)

Answer: C. Most people master a first language (L1), but rarely do they master a second language (L2)
One of the most important things to know about the differences between first language (L1) and second language (L2) acquisition is that people usually will master L1, but they will almost never be fully proficient in L2.

9. **Which statement is an example of specific individual praise?**
(Average) (Skill 3.4)

    A.   "John, you are the only person in class not paying attention"

    B.   "William, I thought we agreed that you would turn in all of your homework"

    C.   "Robert, you did a good job staying in line. See how it helped us get to music class on time"

    D.   "Class, you did a great job cleaning up the art room"

Answer: C. "Robert, you did a good job staying in line. See how it helped us get to music class on time"

Praise is a powerful tool in obtaining and maintaining order in a classroom. In addition, it is an effective motivator. It is even more effective if the praise is specific and the positive results of good behavior are included.

INSTRUCTION AND ASSESSMENT

10. **How can mnemonic devices be used to increase achievement?**
    (Average) (Skill 4.1)

    A. They help students learn to pronounce assigned terms

    B. They provide visual cues to help students recall information

    C. They give auditory hints to increase learner retention

    D. They are most effective with kinesthetic learners

Answer: B. They provide visual cues to help students recall information
Mnemonics rely not only on repetition to remember facts but also on associations between easy-to-remember constructs and lists of data. It is based on the principle that the human mind can more easily recall insignificant data when it is attached (in a logical way) to spatial, personal, or otherwise meaningful information.

11. **Learning centers are unique instructional tools because they allow students to do all of the following except?**
    (Average) (Skill 4.2)

    A. Learn through play

    B. Sit in their seats to complete assignments

    C. Select their own activities

    D. Set up the activity area under a teacher's guidance

Answer: B. Sit in their seats to complete assignments
Learning centers are extremely important in flexible classrooms. In this set-up, students have some time during which they can choose their own activity. Under a teacher's guidance, learners can even create the centers, collecting the necessary items, and then set up the area.

12. Discovery learning is to inquiry as direct instruction is to…
    (Rigorous) (Skill 4.2)

    A. Loosely developed lessons

    B. Clear instructions

    C. Random lessons

    D. Class discussion

Answer: B. Clear instructions
Direct instruction is a teaching method that emphasizes well-developed and carefully planned lessons with small learning increments. It assumes that learning outcomes are improved through clear instruction that eliminates misinterpretations.

13. A computer network includes physical infrastructure such as which of the following?
    (Easy) (Skill 4.4)

    A. Software

    B. Web sites

    C. Operating systems

    D. Cables

Answer: D. Cables
In part, a computer network includes physical infrastructure like wires, cables, fiber optic lines, undersea cables, and satellites.

14. What would improve planning for instruction?
    (Average) (Skill 5.1)

    A. Describing the role of the teacher and student

    B. Assessing the outcomes of prior instruction

    C. Rearranging the order of activities

    D. Giving outside assignments

Answer: B. Assessing the outcomes of prior instruction
It is important to plan the content, materials, activities, and goals of a lesson. However, these steps will not make a difference if students are not able to demonstrate improvement in the skills being taught. Planning frequently misses the mark or fails to allow for unexpected factors. The teacher must constantly adapt all aspects of the curriculum to what is actually happening in the classroom. Effective instruction occurs when the teacher assesses the outcomes regularly and then makes adjustments accordingly.

15. Teachers must use lesson plans to do all of the following except:
    (Rigorous) (Skill 5.1)

    A. Meet specified goals and objectives

    B. Match the lesson to students' abilities and needs

    C. Test a strategy proposed by a research journal

    D. Meet state and local learning standards

Answer: C. Test a strategy proposed by a research journal
Lesson plans must meet specified goals and objectives, it is important to ensure that they match students' abilities and needs. In addition, the lesson's objectives must include state and local expectations.

16. **Norm-referenced tests:**
    (Rigorous) (Skill 6.1)

    A. Provide information about how local test takers performed compared to local test takers from the previous year

    B. Provide information about how the local test takers performed compared to a representative sampling of national test takers

    C. Make no comparisons to national test takers

    D. None of the above

Answer: B. Provide information about how the local test takers performed compared to a representative sampling of national test takers
Norm-referenced tests are designed to measure what a student knows in a particular subject in relation to other students of similar characteristics. They typically provide information about how the local test takers did compared to a representative sampling of national test takers.

17. _____ is a standardized test in which performance is directly related to the educational objective(s)
    (Rigorous) (Skill 6.1)

    A. Aptitude test

    B. Norm-referenced test

    C. Criterion-referenced test

    D. Summative evaluation

Answer: C. Criterion-referenced test
A criterion-referenced test takes the educational objectives of a course and rewrites them in the form of questions. The questions on the test are directly related to the objectives upon which the instruction is based. Thus the results of a criterion-referenced test will tell which objectives of the course a student has mastered and which one he/she has not mastered.

18. Which of the following is the least appropriate reason for teachers to be able to analyze data on their students?
    (Rigorous) (Skill 6.2)

    A. To provide appropriate instruction

    B. To make instructional decisions

    C. To separate students into weaker and stronger academic groups

    D. To communicate and determine instructional progress

Answer: C. To separate students into weaker and stronger academic groups
Especially in today's high stakes environment, it is critical that teachers have a complete understanding of the process involved in examining student data in order to make instructional decisions, prepare lessons, determine progress, and report progress to stakeholders.

19. The seven purposes of assessment, they include all of the following except:
    (Easy) (Skill 6.2)

    A. To identify students' strengths and weaknesses

    B. To assess the effectiveness of a particular instructional strategy

    C. To provide data that assists in decision making

    D. None of the above

Answer: D. None of the above
The seven purposes of assessment are:
- To assist student learning
- To identify students' strengths and weaknesses
- To assess the effectiveness of a particular instructional strategy
- To assess and improve the effectiveness of curriculum programs
- To assess and improve teaching effectiveness
- To provide data that assists in decision making
- To communicate with and involve parents and other stakeholders

COMMUNICATION TECHNIQUES

20. **What has research shown to be the effect of using advance organizers in the lesson?**
(Average) (Skill 7.1)

   A. They facilitate learning and retention

   B. They allow teachers to use their planning time effectively

   C. They only serve to help the teacher organize the lesson

   D. They show definitive positive results on student achievement

Answer: A. They facilitate learning and retention
J. M. Kallison Jr. found that subject matter retention increased when lessons included an outline at the beginning of the lesson and a summary at the end. This type of structure is utilized in successful classrooms and is especially valuable to the visual learner and is a motivational factor for most students.

21. **To facilitate discussion-oriented, non-threatening communication among all students, teachers must do which of the following:**
(Average) (Skill 8.1)

   A. Model appropriate behavior

   B. Allow students to express themselves freely

   C. Show students that some views will not be tolerated

   D. Explain that students should not disagree

Answer: A. Model appropriate behavior
To facilitate discussion-oriented, non-threatening communication among all students, teacher must take the lead and model appropriate actions and speech. They must also intervene quickly when a student makes a misstep and offends another (this often happens inadvertently).

22. **In diverse classrooms, teachers must ensure that they neither protect students from criticism nor praise them because of their ethnicity or gender. Doing either action may result in which of the following outcomes.**
    (Average) (Skill 8.1)

    A. Classmates may become anxious or resentful when dealing with the diverse students

    B. Parents will appreciate their child being singled out

    C. The child will be pleased to receive this attention

    D. Other teachers will follow this example

Answer: A. Classmates may become anxious or resentful when dealing with the diverse students

Don't "protect" students from criticism because of their ethnicity or gender. Likewise, acknowledge and praise all meritorious work without singling out particular students. Both actions can make all students hyper-aware of ethnic and gender differences and cause anxiety or resentment throughout the class.

PROFESSION AND COMMUNITY

23. Teachers should network with one another for all of the following reasons except _____?
    (Average) (Skill 10.1)

    A.   To discuss challenges they face in their classrooms

    B.   To develop a sense of community

    C.   To earn their clock-hours for licensure renewal

    D.   To find solutions to difficult problems

Answer: C. To earn their clock-hours for licensure renewal
Educators have begun to encourage networking for teachers to get together and develop a sense of community. This also allows teachers to discuss what is going on in their classrooms; often just knowing that someone else is encountering the same difficulties is useful. But more than that, talking about the problem will very likely suggest a solution that everyone can take back and use in their own classrooms. Also, some teachers will have focused on a problem more than others and may have found solutions that can be useful. Older teachers can often provide comfort, guidance, and ideas from which young teachers can profit.

24. According to research, one of the greatest obstacles facing new teachers is which of the following?
    (Easy) (Skill 10.3)

    A.   Behavioral issues

    B.   Disagreements with the administration

    C.   Excessive paperwork

    D.   Fending off colleagues who give unwanted advice

Answer: A. Behavioral Issues
Research has shown that for new teachers entering the profession, the two greatest obstacles are dealing with behavioral issues and reaching students who are minimally engaged in their own learning processes

Answer Key

1.	A	13.	D
2.	C	14.	B
3.	B	15.	C
4.	C	16.	B
5.	D	17.	C
6.	A	18.	C
7.	B	19.	D
8.	C	20.	A
9.	C	21.	A
10.	B	22.	A
11.	B	23.	C
12.	B	24.	A

Rigor Table

	Easy 25%	Average 46%	Rigorous 29%
Questions	1, 7, 8, 13, 19, 24	4, 5, 6, 9, 10, 11, 14, 20, 21, 22, 23	2, 3, 12, 15, 16, 17, 18,

Case History

Ms. Jones' Class
Ms. Jones is a new fourth grade teacher. She has 27 students in her class. Her school, Oak Street Elementary, draws from a wide variety of neighborhoods, and the students are very diverse. Some come from impoverished families and others from middle class families. There are almost an equal number of students who are African American, Latino, and White. A small remainder of students is from other racial groups.

The reading curriculum that Ms. Jones must teach is highly prescribed, meaning that over an hour and a half, she must follow the text, with all its activities, closely. Each week, the class typically reads a story together, and most of their activities are related to the story. On Mondays there is a heavy emphasis on vocabulary. Then students read the story for the first time on Tuesdays; they often re-read the story on Wednesday. Or, if it is a longer story, they will read the first half on Tuesday and the second half on Wednesday. Thursdays and Fridays are reserved for writing activities, vocabulary quizzes, graphic organizers, and other synthesizing assignments.

Getting to Know Ms. Jones' Students
Ms. Jones's class is intentionally heterogeneous, meaning that students in the class have varied achievement levels. Two students have been tested as gifted and are part of the school's Gifted and Talented Education program. Three of her students have Individual Educational Plans (IEPs), and one of these three has a behavioral disorder. He came from an abusive family and still suffers from the experience. The other two have Attention Deficit Hyperactivity Disorder.

Ms. Jones realized on the first day of school that some students were quiet and shy, while others were very social and talkative. She also noticed that some students were more motivated than others.

New Teacher Coach Observation Notes - Tuesday, October 14th
I like how Ms. Jones called the class' attention immediately after they returned from recess. She did a good job of getting everyone seated quickly. The students seemed to really know the procedures to get started with reading.

Ms. Jones quickly groups them into pairs. It appears that she has randomly assigned students together. I know two students who have IEPs, and they are together; yet another student with an IEP is matched with a gifted student. I'm not quite sure why she paired students this way.

First, the class reviewed yesterday's vocabulary words. It looks like some of the students do not remember the meanings of the words. I notice that two boys on the far left side of the room are play fighting with their pencils. I don't think Ms. Jones notices this. Ms. Jones says to the class, "Okay, let's start reading the story. Switch off when I flick the lights, okay." One person in each pair is reading aloud, while the other student is supposed to be following along. It looks like some are not. Furthermore, it is very noisy in the room now. I wonder how students are concentrating on the meaning of the story.

She flicks the lights, and students slowly switch to the other reader. It seems like a messy process. Some pairs switch immediately, right in the middle of the sentence; others wait for a more appropriate stopping point. They continue reading for a few minutes, and then Ms. Jones switches readers again.

At the end of the reading, Ms. Jones has a graphic organizer on the board. It is a flow-map. She asks each pair to join the pair next to them to make groups of four. These groups of four work on completing a graphic organizer until the end of reading time. Most groups are working productively, however, some barely finished in time; those who did not finish in time had flow-maps that were incomplete, messy, and occasionally incorrect.

Discussion between Ms. Jones (J) and New Teacher Coach (C) - Later in the Afternoon

C: What did you like about this lesson?

J: Well, I was glad that we got everything done today. I didn't think they'd be able to do both the entire story, as well as the graphic organizer. That's a lot of work for such a short period of time. I know everyone didn't do as well as I would have liked, but most of them did a great job.

C: Well, I'm glad you got everything done, but are you sure that all your students understood the story?

J: I'm pretty sure, as the graphic organizers look good.

C: But you had them in groups; how do you know all students understood?

J: I'm not sure.

C: I'm also wondering how well they knew the vocabulary words from yesterday. What did you do to connect the words to their background knowledge?

J: We did word webs. The students seemed to know the words quite well at the end of reading yesterday. I was surprised to see that some of them forgot the words today. I want to go over the words again tomorrow.

C: That's terrific! Now, did you notice that the boy in the third row, a little to the left, was a little confused? Is he learning English?

J: Oh, yes, that's Christian. He is a native Spanish-speaker. He's doing fine in English, though. I hear him talking in English proficiently with all his friends as if he were a native speaker.

C: Okay, but I'm concerned he did not know what he was reading today.

J: I better check into that.

C: I also noticed that a few groups were not working together well. It seemed that they were arguing over the paper being messy. Do they have strategies for dealing with disagreements in groups?

J: No, but usually, I try to monitor everything carefully. I must not have seen that. If I had, I would have dealt with it.

C: Well, we better end the meeting for the afternoon. Let's talk tomorrow about how we can fix some of these issues. You did great, despite the concerns I brought up. You're going to make a fine teacher!!

Ms. Jones' Teaching Journal - Tuesday, October 14th

There are a few things I'd do differently, but overall, I'm pleased with what happened today. I just don't know how to get through to Kelly. She seems very upset about something; obviously, her reaction to her group about the sloppiness on the paper was uncalled for. I suppose I may need to teach some better group behaviors. I hope to be able to work more closely with Danny. His IEP says he needs extra teacher-time, but I'm really struggling to get that time in there for him.

Question 1

Ms. Jones presented a well-planned lesson and used strong instructional strategies. However, she noticed that not all students responded to the lesson in the way she desired.

- Explain some of the elements of Ms. Jones' class that day that could have been modified to meet the needs of all students.
- Provide recommendations on how Ms. Jones can be guided by learning theories as she makes modifications to her lessons in the future.

Sample Answer

Perhaps Ms. Jones' pacing for this lesson was appropriate; however, she did seem more concerned with getting the work done than ensuring that all students understood what they were reading. First, Ms. Jones never made it clear exactly what her anticipated objectives were for student learning in this day's lesson. While, undoubtedly, she should want for students to have complete comprehension of the story and strong recall of vocabulary words by the end of the week, for the particular day, there is no way to tell what Ms. Jones expected of her students.

If she had a better idea of her expectations, she might have provided further direction to her students on what to look for while reading and what to include in the graphic organizer. Her comment that the "graphic organizers look good" seems to suggest that Ms. Jones had not thought of the end product that she wanted students to produce. One of the primary ways teachers assist students in meeting objectives is by clearly informing them of what is expected and then possibly providing them with a model. The fact that she looked at group-designed graphic organizers does not indicate how well individual students comprehended the story. In addition, the environment may not have been as conducive as possible for intense comprehension and cognitive work. While some students work well with noise, many do not. The interruptions in reading, for example, do not help keep a reading flow alive.

Finally, Ms. Jones should consider lengthening the pacing of the lesson. In that way, groups could work at rates that were appropriate and fewer groups would have rushed to complete the work. By having sufficient time, they avoid hurriedly writing down answers that were possibly incorrect. Some groups certainly will finish sooner than others and Ms. Jones should prepare activities for those groups to complete.

Commentary on Sample Answer

This essay would receive a 2 as it responds to all parts of the question, provides multiple details, and references aspects of learning theory appropriate to the case.

Question 2

Ms. Jones' class is very diverse. She definitely wants to reach all students, but with 27 students in her class, she has to find ways to differentiate her instruction.

- Discuss aspects of Ms. Jones' lesson that could have been better differentiated.
- Provide recommendations using knowledge of classroom management, learning theory, learning English as a second or other language, and learning disabilities.

Sample Answer

The first concern of differentiation is that the groups were not arranged in ways conducive to Ms. Jones' goals for the lesson. While some students were heterogeneously groups, others were not. There did not seem to be a plan for this. While it is important to have occasional homogonous groupings (as in the case where gifted students work together and will finish ahead of the class), heterogeneous groups are positive for many reasons.

First, students with disabilities or those learning English as a second (or other) language can gain a lot by interacting with their peers who are fluent or non-disabled. Second, when fluent and non-disabled students teach concepts to other students, even in informal settings, they make the learning more concrete for themselves. Particularly in the case of second language learners, discussion in a social setting is an effective way of increasing competency. One problem is that Ms. Jones assumed that since Christian sounded fluent with his friends, he was fluent in reading comprehension.

Often, ability for social discussion (referred to as Basic Interpersonal Communication Skills) is obtained far sooner than academic language skills (referred to as Cognitive Academic Language Proficiency). Ms. Jones may want to pair Christian with students she knows will assist his academic language development. In terms of the students with learning disabilities, Ms. Jones should spend more time with them (as she notes in her journal). However, if she pairs them with other students who can assist them, she will only have to check in on them occasionally but not have to sit with them throughout the entire lesson. Finally, in regard to students who were off-task, Ms. Jones can simply walk around the room more often, checking in on work, listening to students as they read, and being "proximal" to ward off behavior that exists due to a teachers' physical absence.

Commentary on Sample Answer

This answer would receive a score of 2. It effectively combines classroom management and differentiation strategies with learning and language theories. It provides specific examples that demonstrate knowledge of how to apply those theories to classroom practice.

Question 3

Ms. Jones was concerned about the fact that some students had forgotten many of the words they studied yesterday.

- Discuss the importance of learning new concepts and vocabulary in context.
- Provide examples of how Ms. Jones might extend the students' learning of vocabulary throughout the week.

Sample Answer

People do not learn concepts or terms immediately upon hearing them. Retention requires repeated exposure, preferably in natural settings. In terms of vocabulary, a natural setting is one in which there is context. Thus, instead of providing a list of words for students to remember, students learn the words in the context of a story. Now, the case history did mention that Ms. Jones had: 1. "frontloaded" the words the day before reading the story; 2. worked to connect the words to students' background knowledge; and 3. used word webs to integrate their understandings of the words. However, the first time the students read the story, on the day of the observed lesson, there was no reference to the words they studied the day before.

Although undoubtedly some students would have known them from the previous day—and others would simply have recognized them—there was no attempt from Ms. Jones to review them on their first encounter with the words in a natural context. To extend their learning of those words, Ms. Jones should review them in the context of the story. This will help in two ways. First, it will provide a better opportunity for them to learn the words based on their understanding of the story. Second, by reviewing potentially difficult words, their understanding of the story may be increased. Lastly, Ms. Jones might also extend their learning by having students relate the meaning of the words in the story to events or experiences from their own lives. She will also want to re-visit those words multiple times during the week of the lesson and in subsequent lessons to ensure they have multiple exposures to the words.

Commentary on Sample Answer

This answer would receive a 2 because it successfully integrates theories of background knowledge and contextual learning with specific instructional

Case History

Scenario

Terrace Park Elementary has a tradition of assigning research reports in every class from grades two to six. In grades two and three, students explore topics and write paragraphs to demonstrate their new learning. In grades four and five, students learn conventions of research reports and practice using libraries and the Internet to do research. In fifth grade, students write a short report on a U.S. state. In grade six, students have to integrate all their knowledge of research reports and write a report on a U.S. president of their choice.

Mr. Michaels has taught sixth grade at Terrace Park for a few years. He has analyzed all aspects of his teaching each year and made changes to improve in subsequent years. His approach to this research report unit is no different; since this is the pinnacle of the sixth grade at Terrace Park, Mr. Michaels wants to make this project the finest instructional experience students have ever had at the school.

The Professional Learning Community of Terrace Park

All upper grade teachers at Terrace Park Elementary meet together every other week to plan lessons, discuss units, and design assessments. They often look at student learning data to guide their practices. Now that the teachers are getting ready to start the research report assignment in each of their classes, Mr. Michaels has compiled data from last year's assignment and developed tentative plans for this year's assignment. Other teachers have also brought in data and lesson plans.

During the planning meetings, teachers first examine the work of their current students when they were in the previous grade. So, Mr. Michaels spends this meeting looking at his students' fifth grade state reports. He also discusses his students' performance with their fifth grade teacher, Ms. Johnson.

Conversation between Ms. Johnson (J) and Mr. Michaels (M) - Prior to Starting the Research Assignment

J: I think you're going to find that your students really enjoy researching presidents. I'm not so sure that you'll be impressed with their skills in researching and writing reports. I know last year was the first time they had learned how to evaluate sources on the Internet, but I really don't think they got it at all.

M: That's okay. I plan on spending considerable time with that this year. What things did they master in terms of developing research skills?

J: Well, in the fourth grade, they had learned how to use the index of books. They really built on that skill last year. I doubt you'll have to spend much time on that. Last year, we spent a lot of time on learning how to summarize and paraphrase the research they find. However, I would argue that they have a lot of extra work to do with that, just because it is so hard. At this point, I really couldn't tell you how well they will do; all I know is that we spent a lot of time on it.

M: What about the writing of the reports? How well did they do with that?

J: Well, as you know, their skills in writing are all over the place. I think about half the class is at standard, one quarter below standard, and one quarter way above standard. It makes it very tough to teach to all students.

M: I hear you there! Thanks for all your advice!

From Mr. Michaels' Lesson Plan Journal - Prior to Starting the Research Assignment

I have yet to decide how I want to group students. I know that I am going to have to group them heterogeneously. I also know that I want to teach many concepts such as using graphic organizers to plan writing, assist in reading bibliographies, and revising writing. I don't know whether I should completely re-teach summarization, as Ms. Johnson did spend a lot of time on that. I'm a little concerned about some of the students who plagiarized on their science reports last fall. Maybe I should lay out the rules on plagiarism again. What I really want to focus on, though, is critical thinking. Unfortunately, the last time I did a critical thinking lesson, I don't think it went over very well. Finally, I hope I can find enough resources online and at the school library. I'll just jump into this and see where it takes me!!

A Day in the Life of Mr. Michaels' Writing Workshop - Half-way Into the Research Report Assignment

Students are in writing groups. Mr. Michaels just finished a mini-lesson on the differences between passive and active voice. In writing groups, Mr. Michaels has asked his students to read each others' papers and identify areas where passive voice could be changed to active voice. In one group, some students clearly did not understand the lesson and are now making other corrections to each others' papers, such as spelling. Mr. Michaels did not work with this group, as he assumed they were working on active and passive voice. One student in another group seemed to be struggling with coming up with an active version of a passive sentence. The rest of his group has left him behind as the rest of them seemed proficient with the concept. Since most of the class did understand the work for the day, Mr. Michaels' is concerned about whether or not he should return to this lesson the next day or move on.

Question 1

Clearly, Mr. Michaels wanted to understand where his students were prior to beginning this unit of instruction. He wanted to make sure he was starting at an appropriate instructional level.

- What additional areas could Mr. Michaels have investigated before planning this unit? What types of additional data could he have used to drive instruction?
- How could Mr. Michaels better monitor students' learning throughout the unit so that he is constantly aware of where they are? Base your answer on principles of instructional planning and assessment.

Sample Answer

While Mr. Michaels examined student work and talked to the fifth grade teacher, undoubtedly, in the current year, students have learned many things from him. The information from the fifth grade project will be helpful in terms of aligning instruction vertically. However, Mr. Michaels might want to do a pre-assessment prior to developing the unit so he can get a feel for the specific areas on which he should concentrate. He may have had the curriculum in mind, as well as state standards and assessments; however, he might have spent more time reviewing the specific expectations required of his students. This would certainly assist his students on achievement tests, and more importantly, it would allow them to go into seventh grade having mastered the standards required of them by the state and district.

Finally, in terms of assessing readiness, Mr. Michaels should examine multiple sources of data, including his classroom assessments in history (as the research is history-based), writing, and reading. Reading scores alone would tell him a lot about the types of things he might do to help them comprehend texts with difficult information. During the unit, Mr. Michaels obviously should have assessed their skills by examining their work according to rubrics or scoring guides. This would allow him to objectively mark their progress. His assumption that because they did not ask for assistance, his students were understanding the lesson, was incorrect. In writing workshops, teachers can meet with students briefly to read their writing and give feedback orally. This takes less time than writing extensive comments, and the oral feedback can be more memorable and personal to students as they go back and revise.

Commentary on Sample Answer

This answer would receive a score of 2, as it addresses all concerns regarding the use of data prior to planning. It also effectively provides examples, supported by theory, as to how Mr. Michaels can monitor his students' progress throughout the unit.

Question 2

Mr. Michaels was concerned about student plagiarism. He also expressed confusion over whether to re-teach skills such as summarization. Ms. Johnson suggested that the students did not have enough time to learn the skills of evaluating research sources, particularly from the Internet.

- Provide recommendations for Mr. Michaels as he decides instructional areas to focus on for this unit. Base your answers on knowledge of curriculum, instructional planning, and student learning.

Sample Answer

While many students who plagiarize realize that they are being dishonest, some students actually do not know how to summarize or paraphrase. They turn to plagiarizing often because they know of no other way to present research from the materials that they read. Mr. Michaels could first provide a pre-test of summarization and paraphrasing. To do so, he could give students a sample passage from an encyclopedia, for example, and ask them to summarize the article first, then paraphrase it. Even though there is a distinction between the two and even though he is attempting to assess their prior knowledge, it would still be a good idea for Mr. Michaels to remind students of the differences between summarization and paraphrasing.

Once he sees samples of what the students understand from summarizing and paraphrasing—and how well they are able to do both—he can then decide how long to focus on the topic. Instead of assuming that students will not plagiarize just because they know the rules, Mr. Michaels can help the students learn practical strategies to help them summarize and paraphrase more effortlessly. Since these skills are strategies that students can use—and apply to other similar activities—Mr. Michaels should teach them explicitly. While he may not have to completely re-teach these skills, he could certainly re-visit them, as well as build upon them by adding more complex techniques. Just because students learn the skills at a basic level does not mean that they will naturally transfer the learning to more advanced stages of the skills. Finally, Mr. Michaels can teach students the skills of summarization and paraphrasing by using Internet sources. While learning the skills of summarization, as applied to online information, students will also learn how to evaluate sources of information, as that type of differentiation is a central part of summarization.

Commentary on Sample Answer

This response would earn a score of 2. It blends creative and efficient instructional principals with theories of learning and skill-based inquiry.

Question 3

Mr. Michaels has some concept of what he wants students to do with this report, but he did say, "I'll just jump into this and see where it takes me."

- What problems might arise with this approach?
- How can Mr. Michaels retain the ability to utilize "teachable moments" while still holding students accountable to a clearly defined standard? Base your answer on theories of learning and assessment

Sample Answer

All lesson planning and unit planning should be driven by expected outcomes and assessments. Instructional design theory suggests that assessments should be designed *before* lesson plans are written. In that way, teachers *and* students will have a clear picture of what needs to be taught and learned. The goal of instruction, then, is getting students from where they are to the standard set forth by the grading criteria of the final assessment.

In Mr. Michaels' case, the final assessment is the completed research paper. Throughout the unit he may want to judge how students are progressing and then adjust instruction accordingly. He should have a clearly defined curriculum map that outlines all the components necessary to get students from where they are at the beginning of the unit to the final assessment, the completed research report. By just jumping into it, Mr. Michaels may end up feeling burdened by all the skills that he needs to teach. When they feel overwhelmed, many teachers often fail to seriously reinforce many skills, and often teach them poorly.

If, however, Mr. Michaels realizes he can only teach a finite amount of skills, and then adjusts his expectations on the final assessment accordingly, he will most likely teach his selected skills in greater depth. In this way, while students may not learn everything, they will have learned certain things better. Furthermore, he might build in extra time for review, for "teachable moments", and for unexpected circumstances.

In summary, having a road map will help him stay on target better than if he were to just plunge into the unit. What makes a curriculum-map approach better is that it gives the teacher and the students' direction and bite-sized pieces of learning. Too much at one time is sure to confuse students. Many students, as well, will not respond successfully to a barrage of skills thrown at them; they really do need careful guidance, in-depth practice, and clear direction.

Commentary on Sample Answer
This response would earn a 2 because it demonstrates a clear connection of assessment and instructional theory to classroom practices and unit design.

www.ingramcontent.com/pod-product-compliance
Lightning Source LLC
LaVergne TN
LVHW061319060426
835507LV00019B/2234